The Dolphins

Story by Rose Inserra
Illustrations by Meredith Thomas

NELSON PRICE MILBURN

"I don't want to go out
with Dad today," said Jason.
"I want to go to Ben's place
and practise my swimming in his pool."

"Your dad will be disappointed,"
Mum told him.
"He's taking you for a special swim.
I think you should go."

Jason didn't want to disappoint his dad.
He only spent time with him on Saturdays.

When Jason heard Dad's car horn,
he ran outside.

"Hi, Dad. Where are we going today?"
Jason asked.

"We're going to Seaport
for a special swim," said Dad.

"What kind of a special swim?" asked Jason.

"You'll see," replied Dad. "It's a surprise."

Jason sighed.
He really wanted to swim in Ben's pool.
The sea had waves and seaweed.
He could swim much better in a pool.

It was hot and stuffy in Dad's car,
and the seats were sticky under his legs.
"We'll be there soon," said Dad.

The cars on the road were moving slowly.
Fumes from the traffic
made Jason feel sick.
The trip seemed to be taking forever.

Finally they came over a hill
and Jason could see the sea.
"Nearly there," said Dad.

Dad drove into the car park near the pier.
But the car park was full.
"We'll have to park further away," said Dad.
Jason said nothing.

Dad drove around for ages.
At last, he found a parking spot,
but it was a long way from the pier.
Dad and Jason began the hot walk back.
"When are we going
to have the special swim, Dad?" asked Jason.

Dad pointed to the end of the pier.
"See that boat? It will take us
to the special swimming place," he said.

Jason just nodded.

Dad and Jason finally reached
the end of the pier.
A woman wearing a wetsuit
was waiting near the boat,
and so were some other people.

"Hi, I'm Judy," she said.
"I'll be coming out with you today as your instructor.
Time to go," she called. "All aboard!"

Dad and Jason sat together on the deck. They watched Judy handing out wetsuits, masks and snorkels.

"What's all this for?" asked Jason.

"We'll need this special gear," said Dad, pulling on his wetsuit.

"We are going on a dolphin swim!"

Dolphins! That **was** a surprise!
Jason listened as Judy told everyone
the rules for swimming with dolphins.

"There will be two ropes trailing
out behind the boat," Judy said.
"To be safe in the water
you must hold onto a rope at all times.
Don't kick or splash,
because that could frighten the dolphins.
If they swim near you,
don't touch them.
Just let them swim around you."

Jason looked out to sea, hoping that
he would be the first to see a dolphin.

He couldn't see anything except blue sky
and white capped waves.

"The dolphins are usually here by now,"
said Judy. "I do hope they come today.
They don't always come."

Jason made a face.
So much for the special swim!
There'd be no need
to get into the water at all
if the dolphins didn't come.

Jason looked into the distance.
He thought he saw
something move above the waves,
far behind the boat.

Whatever it was, it disappeared
behind a big wave.

Suddenly Jason saw a dolphin leap
high out of the water.
And then he saw another and another.

"Wow!" Jason cried.
"The dolphins are here!"

All the people on the boat stood up to look.

"We'll stop the boat," shouted Judy.
"Everyone, get ready to go in."
Judy slipped into the water first
from the back of the boat.
"I'll swim with you," she said to Jason.

Jason slid into the water.
He grabbed the rope
and let it run through his hands
until he drifted out to Judy.

Jason put his face down into the water.
He saw a moving grey shape.

The dolphin seemed to be smiling
as it rolled over to one side.
Closer and closer it came
until its fin almost tickled his tummy.
Then it swam away under the boat.

Jason held his breath.
The dolphin had come so close!

Jason lifted his head out of the water and looked around for Dad.

"How was that for a swim?" asked Dad, who was back on the boat taking photos.

"A dolphin nearly touched me," shouted Jason. "It was **excellent**, Dad!"